Bird with a Bright Object

AmyLee

Copyright © 2024 by AmyLee

All rights reserved.

No portion of this book may be reproduced in any form without written permission from the publisher or author, except as permitted by U.S. copyright law.

Cover Artwork and Design by Kathrine Magpie Design

Interior Design by Jourdan Dunn

Table of Contents

Tales from Life

Invitation	1
Blue is for Memory	3
Safety	4
Truth	5
Cat Toy	7
Consent	9
Consider	10
Keep Me Honest	11
Easy Words	12
Finish	13
Frozen	14
Haunted	15
Irresponsible	16
Jealousy	18
Sail	19
Mute	20
Nervous	21
Skin	22
Suitable	23
Vent	24
You Shall See Wonders	25

Family

The Art of Naming Flowers	29
Blue Jays	32
Time for Mending	34
Best Worst Dog	36
Twitch	38
Feathers for Bird	39
Found	40
Gene Vincent	42

God Only Knows	44
Snowshoe Springs	46
What Would the Neighbors Say	48
Red Motorcycle	49
Rain Always Brings You Back	51

Ancestors

Unwilling Subjects	55
Eulogy	57
California Cowboys	59
Children at a Birthday Party	62
Walking on Kingsbury Grade	64

Grief Wears Many Faces

I Want to Know You	69
Familiar	70
Orange Geraniums	71
Silence	72
Two Years, Seven Months, Two Days	73
Lost Years	75
When I'm Done	78

Glorious Nature

Breathe	81
Dragonfly Season	83
Lavender and Bees	85
A Realization of Spiders	87
Bee Hives	89
Nesting Box	91
Damselfly	93
Cracked Open	94
Flow	95
Smoke Cherry	96
Conversations with Gravity	97

Filled with Joy	99
Lightning Rod	101
Run Free	102
Stormy Skies	103
The Element of Water	105
First Time	106
Brittle	107
When I Feel Most Alive	108
Wild Fire	109

There is No Light Without Darkness

Barest Concessions	113
Elevator	115
When It Comes to You	117
Nothing	119
Overheard Conversation	120
After Las Vegas	121
Dormant	123
Heirlooms	124
Judgment	126

Mon Ami, Mon Amour

Early Morning Light	129
My Favorite Place	130
Jolly Rancher	131
Fnar	132
Heart of Desire	133
This Poem is a Secret	134
Broken	135
Yearning	136
Honey Mead	137
Spark	139
Navigating Bodies	140
Broken-Hearted	141
Forbidden Fruit	143
House	144

My Wish for You	146
It Breaks You	147
Proper	148
Sharp Edges	149
Tough Love	150
Mojave	151

See Me

Duality	155
You Were Born with Wings	156
Incantation	157
Mythical Creatures	158
Poetic Faith	160
Leap of Faith	161
All About Poems	162
Beautiful Reminder	163
I wish	164
Fairy Tale	166
My Body as a Fortress	168
Don't Let Them See	169
New Beginning	170
Pretty Girls	171
Task Completed	172
Anyone's Goddess	173
Trust in Dreams	174
The Woman in the Mirror	175
Where Creativity Flows	176
Dreams	178
I Walked a Wooded Path	180
See Me	181
International Women's Day	182
Sprout	183

This book of poetry is dedicated to my dear birdie girl.
Thank you for believing in me.
Love you with all my heart and soul, Mom.

Savor and enjoy the company of AmyLee's poems. She presents them for you to read and ponder. *Bird with a Bright Object* is a journey through her many lives. Let this poet guide you from one phase to the next in a deeply revealing expression of how and why she became the gifted creative she is today.

– R.A. Steele

Tales from Life

Invitation

This chaotic life
rarely subtle
but I will
make room
make sure
souls find
safe places
in me

Shelter and comfort
for those who need it
whether they know it or not

A place of rest from
life and struggles
you are invited
to taste
simple warmth

I live
where solitude is ruler
and I quite like the echoes

If you need quarter
to recharge
consider this your succor

Find your hugs
bide your time
watch the birds
feel sunrise
and sunset

I will help you slow down
you can free your mind
of that which plagues you

Because my friend
these things
I desperately need too
much as I love
my peace and the great quiet
on existential shores
I'd rather do them
with a friend, a companion, a love

If we put our hearts together
what can we make of today.

Blue is for Memory

My interior life is pairing memories
With a pretty box of crayons
And that satisfied feeling when
One matches perfectly
What I see in my imagination

There is Parrish blue
The color of sky
And clouds in the gloaming
Johnson's Blue Geranium
A special fondness of our Mary
Cobalt blue pretties in Mama's curio case
The shifting blues of summer
Days that stretched forever
My old blue coat on Easter Sunday
Smelling of mothballs and waiting
Buttons like candy disks
Iridescent Lapis jewels to lick
Metal tinned blueberries
Top cheesecake from a box
Love-in-a-Mist running wild
A garden from long ago
Someday, when we meet again
It will be in our blue heaven
My blue eyes are now blue-grey
Once upon a time, they were baby blue
Crying in the rain
It's just the blues
Your blues and my blues
Oh, those blues.

Safety

There have been moments
of fleeting safety
a transitory state of being
a raft floating on
warm water currents
clinging in silent stoicism
to its rough timbers
asylum a wayward stalwart stranger
I drift toward atolls, then islands
seeking, searching, solace
coastlines and continents
as fortitude ripens
assurance creates
pangean landmasses
having gone backward in time
into my dreams
to my very inception
and I am but a genetic code
in someone else's lifetime.

Truth

Where I cannot
ignore
the duality of
my being

Proclaim my truth
face frightened fire
the dread of
aloneness
and angst
not good-ness

My tears are real
as yours
my needs
luminous or opaque
my dreams
are rivers
cold and rushing
calm shallows and warmth

This unease
how it wants to own me
and deign to smother
those sacred places in my spirit
should have, cannot have
must do, frightened to

Every moment
I tarry from
purpose and path
a moment
closer to death

My frail disposition begs you
notice me
then shrinks
from candle's flare
and also hurts
when you do not notice me
an apt excuse for me to hide away

My truth is an unending song
of contradiction
it is all worlds
and each side battles.

Cat Toy

Pain is a thing with wings
or the sails
of a tall ship
it catches hurt
like it catches air
uses it to do its bidding

History with no rhyme or reason
a salty drop of water
a single tear
the sound of alarm and voices harsh
taste of copper in the blood
and bitter pills
smell of dinner burned
of booze, of cigarettes

Memory and things
they say never happened
reading words that comfort
those that frighten

Jaw crosses
eyes narrow
mouth turns down
breathing rasps
before things fall apart

Today it visited
wanting
disguised
felt just as it did
when I was young
I didn't have any answers

it made my soul
catch in my throat
feelings of wrongness
despair, being alone

And then
come to find out
it was just a cat toy
a wrong assumption
again.

Consent

We did not discuss consent
It wasn't the way of the world
Back then
I've done things and had things done
That I will never
Be able to erase from my mind
I did not understand
I had the power to say no.

Consider

Consider, please
The power of your words
How they refract light from the stars
How they echo endlessly in a child's ears
How they sharpen the knife, or dull the senses
Your words contain the power
Consider.

Keep Me Honest

Keep me honest
gods, keep me honest
and pull me up short
if you ever catch me
humble-bragging
the idea makes me
shudder, shiver
solemnly swear
I hate it as much
as the idea
of being precious or twee
but I'm human
so I'm bound to fuck up
but when I do, please
clip my wings.

Easy Words

I worry
my words
may come too easily
that my effortless
jottings
cheapen the overall import
am I too cavalier
too brash
too quick
to make my mark
will I be punished
in some afterlife
of a wordless hellscape.

Finish

I grew up
believing
it was bad
not to finish
my peas or
if I stopped
a thing
that wasn't
my cuppa tea
was I supposed
to be
a famous musician
or Olympic gymnast
what if, instead
we give
ourselves
freedom
to explore notions
that set our
hearts afire.

Frozen

I can still
Remember
How it felt
When my tears
Froze to my cheeks
Touching them
To see if they were real
How strange
Knowing my body
Had become cold enough
For this to be possible.

Haunted

What hunts you down
Keeps you awake
What interrupts sleep and dreams
Awakens you in a sweat
Heartbeat raging
What quickens your breath
First panting, then desperation
What makes you cry out
Alone and afraid
Icy fingers whisper
Up and down your spine
Frozen, afraid to move
Arms held tight across chest
In a barren attempt at safety
From harm or whatever may lurk
In unreliable shadows.

Irresponsible

Think about our little lives and laugh
Always overdrawn, always out of gas, nothing in the fridge
They said we worry about you
And they probably should
We were deliriously naive and madly in love
All those Friday nights—charades, spaghetti, cheap beer
It was all we could afford, felt good, so did we
Parties on Broadway, wild turkey, my god
Evening hadn't even begun, and we were ready to go
Scandalous nights, music at The Lucky Lion
When we hit the Keystone in Berkeley, pure adrenaline
Unbelievably irresponsible

Not overly concerned about right or wrong
When margaritas are flowing
I can tell you from experience
It's never a good idea to cut a friend's hair
Life made from momentary desire
Filled with pleasure, endless fun
Lake Oroville, remember the bonfire
Woke up in the dirt alone, no idea how it happened
Masters of the Universe doll clutched in my hand
Ending up on the back of Eddie's Harley
Taking turns too fast, hangover threatening me
Ridiculously irresponsible

Fishing at the Mothball fleet
It must have been one in the morning
And I had to pee over the side of the boat
But we caught an enormous sturgeon
Holy smokes, they barbeque nice
Strangled anxiety with cigarettes and white Russians
Hiking in the rain, naked in the caves on Mt Diablo

Drinks at Nepenthe's, camping at Big Sur
In a moldy canvas tent that had seen better days
Homeless logger deep in the Rogue River backwoods
Invited for beer and shared his fire, probably wasn't smart, but we lived to tell it
Deliciously irresponsible

Laughed ourselves hysterical at the Sirloin Steak and Brew
Ten dollars, all you can eat, all we could afford, beer included
Splitting traffic through the mountains
Cut-offs, tank top, no helmet, big-ticket, no bathroom
Guys from New Zealand met at Half Moon Bay
Flopped with us for a week
They left me with an accent and a lot of good memories
Yeah, it was time they moved on
You know, it really was okay back then
Fly-by-night and so goddamned free
We were children with no idea what was ahead
Outrageously irresponsible

Jealousy

I am not a thing
I said
To ever inspire feelings
Of possession
Or jealousy
Covetous feelings
Pshaw, sir
Something to lust after
Certainly not
Are my paltry cerebral pursuits
Sexy.
Do they give you shivers.

Sail

We called it flying
round the world
harnesses
clipped and secured
wetsuits - sunglasses
hot chocolate - cigars
choppy fast waters
creating suspension
dangerous tension
breezes and gusts
delicate whirlwinds dance
just above surface
turbulent exhilaration
salted lips
hair, face, and eyes
sun-stripped and bare
elemental alchemy
explorers and pirates
metal bits ringing out
songs drifting on air
mast, sails, rigging
speed and trampoline
power wielded
then dropped overboard
45-degree pontoon
wind sucked from sails
water heaved from lungs
scramble and splutter
we're okay - we're okay.

Mute

Manna flows
words spill from me
good - bad
wrong words
it still flows
I skim
quickly
rearrange something
useful
I do this afraid
if even one
letter is lost
one word goes
astray
my inattention
punished
I will be rendered mute.

Nervous

I'm feeling superstitious
Like, I need some charm
For luck, or wisdom
Some assurance, you see
Because perhaps I've been
Too cocky
At home in the spotlight
Not enough
Humility
Too much conceit
Maybe that, maybe those
Because I swear by the stars
In the nighttime sky
I worry all this magic
Isn't real, and I'm going to
Wake up one day and see
Myself for the pretender I am
My good fortune will run out
If I'm not careful
I'll be stripped of all I know
Along with the love and tender
Feelings
And these notions
They make me nervous.

Skin

My plan was
write something bold
freedom, skin, body politics
but I don't have
energy to fight
a society
insisting
I'm responsible for making a man
feel better about himself
I'm goddamn exhausted
trying to
to argue morals with
a stranger.

Suitable

Hey!
And goddamn
Some days I just want
To be seen, to be real, to be enough
And do I really have to work so hard for it?
How does it work for the lucky ones, the pretty ones?
I don't know, I'll never know, I'm just me, and I'm not suitable.

Vent

When I was newly healing
I had a box
in the basement
and safety glasses
old dishes, cups, saucers
burnt-out light bulbs
made loads of noise
whilst breaking
I'd smash and scream
uncaring of the sounds
vent until I had no more
and felt the high release.

You Shall See Wonders

Life and death
I have seen it more times
would not have thought possible
had I not been there
and those things were miraculous
but what I want to know
what I hope you can tell me, please
what happens before life
and
what happens after death
I suspect many things
but have never seen, never been given
any answer that satisfied me

Do our little soul spirits wait patiently for
birth and choose where they will go
and if this is true, I rail at the
destination for some
the hunger, abuse, and neglect
surely a pure being wouldn't choose that lot
oh, you say, we go where the lessons are
where we have cosmic work to complete
probability of coexistence
I howl and thunder at that, too

Oh, death
I have seen you, breathed, and kissed you
sat next to you on the side of a mountain
and ridden with you
in the back seat of a station wagon
my soft places want to continue
the conversation well after the ashes have cooled
but my hard places shout - at the end, there is nothing

and I weep

I awaken before dawn with
the ancestors prattling - noisily
telling me, I'd best tend to the here and now.

Family

The Art of Naming Flowers

When I was a little girl
Mama trained me in the art of naming flowers
We wandered through the yard
She'd tell me the names
Of everything growing and alive
Year after year
I repeated those words back
And they became my poem, prayer, and promise

Naming flowers was passed from
Great-great-great-grandmother
To younger generations of girls in the family
Finally, that knowledge came down to me
Mama taught her personal flower catechism

The little white flowers low to the ground
Honey-scented Alyssum
Cheerful Zinnias, pink and red and yellow
Steadfast orange marigolds.

I'd repeat all of the names
Using tricks she taught
Each flower was sacred and came with a story

Nasturtiums that crept and climbed
Over the ground and up the fence posts
Twining morning glories opened to greet the day
Mounds of baby tears rested
Low and cool and shady
Grape Hyacinth and Crocus pushed bravely
Through rain-damp soil
Snowball bush towered over the back fence
And made magical snowstorms

Canna, Nile, and Calla - a paradise for snails.
Geraniums scattered out back -
Such forgiving plants -
Bright punctuation marks

Japanese maple
Favorite of climbing cats and small children
This tree required a spring haircut
But wild and shaggy, I loved it best
The details of its leaves
Sunlight dappled and illuminated delicate veins.

Mama turned my hands palm up
So I could compare my own veins and lines
She quietly taught me
The connection we shared with all living things

Cherry tree got disease and died
Leaving a sad spot in the garden
I recall lying underneath on soft grass
Or climbing a little way up its trunk
To get a better view
Of sweet dangling fruits
Before the birds got at them
Meyer lemon tree was in love with the bees
The scent and taste, rich and sweet
Foretelling happiness, pies, and lemon curd
Beneath a beautiful yellow climbing rose
Our Yellow Rose of Texas
I planted Johnny Jump-ups
Just to see their little faces and pretend
They were tiny flower people

The women in my mother's family
Were avid gardeners
By need and design
And taught generations
To love working in the dirt

And making something beautiful with nature.

Blue Jays

Scrub Jay and Steller's Jay
Were your birds, and familiars
Their bright eyes
Recognized your gaze
Flashing
Knowing
Heads cocked in wonder

You showed the world
Tough, stubborn, grumpy
Intractable, irascible
Set in your ways
You were not perfect
So far from perfect
My god
What would you say next
We held our breath
Just waiting
For the shoe to drop

I saw you clearly
How you peeled my grapes
And tried to keep me
Safe from harm
How you showed me
To plant and sow
And tended to the ground
We walked upon
How you were saddled with the job
As my stand-in dad
And never once
Shirked your duty
You left cantaloupe rinds

For birds and squirrels
And built a swing
For playing and dreaming
Taught me to love
In your own strange way
In the afterlife, your soul is divided
Between the Scrub and the Steller's Jay
How could creator make you choose
You worked so hard your whole life
It only seems fair
That you should now inhabit both.

Time for Mending

My little hands
reached into the basket
pulled out things with rips and tears
the mending began
my nana must have had
the patience of a saint
when I was five
she taught me

Buttons, hems
seams gone bad
choose the threads
with care and intent
and the needle must be just right
each stitch same as
the one before and after
lined up perfectly
for maximum satisfaction

Granddaughter
look at my work; it's perfect
you cannot tell the thing
needed fixing in the first place
as lovely inside as out
perfectly disguised damage

There's a lesson
the teaching
or the metaphor
I untangle the knots

Have you seen MY stitches
crooked

a little uneven
threads dangling
but the mending
takes shape as should
I've repaired
dangerous curves
uphill rises

I cannot look at a sewing basket
without thinking of my nana
and how she gave me power over
things that came to be in
my hands

There are wells of loneliness
and unemptied baskets of
torn shirts and missing buttons
grasp one gently but firmly between
your fingers and begin
fix what needs fixing
mend your fences
mind your manners
join what's torn
repair what's broken
pray for salvage.

Best Worst Dog

We brought you home
To cheer up Old Lab
Who was a melancholy baby
He loved you immediately
Already 7 years old, you'd been left
In the no-kill shelter
Longer than they wanted
Because you were so damn sweet
The moment we brought you
To your forever home
You ran out the back door
Killed a baby bird
It had fallen from the nest
Proud of yourself
So willing to please
Then we found out you were a nervous pee-er
You peed everywhere
No matter how many times we walked you
Or let you outside to go
The vet found nothing wrong
So, we coped and loved you
Mostly with kindness and patience
Sometimes with utter frustration and a few harsh words
You and Old Lab loved nothing better
Than to curl up on the couch together
Spooning, yawning, and stretching
And sometimes escape to take yourself out
On unsanctioned walkies
In spite of your plumbing problems
You were the sweetest girl ever
You held up your end of the bargain
And we tried to hold up ours
Until one night, on a neighborhood walk

Your seizures became too much
And I knew it was time -
Beyond time
We'd had you 11 years
You were tired and old
You more than earned your pure and peaceful rest.

Twitch

Safely as
he sleeps
dreams deep
pack leader
running free
grassy fields
eyes blink, roll
sightless now
muscles twitch
flex and bunch
little growl
smallest whimper
is he prey
or is he chasing.

Feathers for Bird

I called you bird
When you were hours old
And bird, you shall always be
You dreamed of feathers
And flight and bright things
And collected diligently

Your five-year-old hands
Carefully crafted
A tiny fantastical car
A gift for tooth fairy, you said
As she made her magical rounds
From star to star to star

You glued parrot's feathers
Up one side and down the other
And made a tiny nest for her
I wish I'd appreciated
The scope of your mind
To better nurture the creator you are

And helped you shine your light stronger
In a world that can be mostly dark
I love how you are, my birdie girl
Please, I beg, do not doubt me
Hear me out – you're perfectly perfect
No matter who you are.

Found

Two girls
Different and same
One was you, and one was me
We had our moods
Lives in need of excavation
Truth in our veins
Silt washed from specks of gold
Painful, hidden, glittering

I took a winding path to find you
And on it, I found myself

More fragile than we cared to admit
Stronger than we imagined
Our troubles
Mountains of stone
Turned to rubble, dirt, ash
Blown to bits
Our very beings
Assembled from the particles
Reformed into shiny ideas
Thoughts become and then, done
When I prayed for blessed peace
You were beside me

Slivers of a lifetime
Or two or many
Someday together again
As the moments
Lengthen to minutes
Become hours
Days and years
Breathe in regrets

Breathe out love
Watch carefully
Over our shoulders
As the miles
Are gobbled whole
It goes so fast
There is comfort
Mama, I found us.

Gene Vincent

Memory plays on repeat
scratchy sound and dust on the needle
in the living room where
some memories are good

And some are not
some are terrible
this one was good
before tough love

It was nighttime, past my bedtime
I can tell by the quality of light
we were dancing, listening to
music on our old record player

Mama in striped peddle-pushers
and a little brown sweater
hair in curlers
me in the dreaded foot pajamas
braids crooked
big sister with a beehive hairdo
frosty white lipstick

Daddy and brother must be out at scouts
for us to be so wild at night
when he was home, things were different
Roger Miller, Chet Atkins, Herb Alpert
Burl Ives, Johnny Cash
good music really
played while sitting respectfully
reading Neville Shute

There was Gene Vincent

Be-Bob-A-Lu-la, she's my baby,
we twisted and shout-sang
"my ba-by love, my ba-by love"
sister rolled her teenaged eyes -
"I have to practice my dance"
one, two, cha, cha, cha
very, very important
three, four, cha, cha, cha

"Let me; I want to."
"There's no room, Amy -
it's my turn - Mom, do something."
And, soon, it would end
with her snit
my tears, my wailing

My thumb in my mouth
little legs swinging angrily off the big chair
then the clouds would part
laughter again
back to the dancing
jumped down, ecstatic, loud
braids dancing, feet dancing
Mama was our referee
"Linda, teach me to Pony. Amy, you do it, too."

God Only Knows

Say my prayers,
recite the psalms
will sleep bring sweet dreams,
or visions of a tortured Christ

Sunday's church, wooden bench hurts,
scrawny legs swinging, socks slipping down,
scuffed Mary-Jane's
if I do it right, will Jesus save...me?

When I talk to God, I'm not sure he listens
would I hear voices if my angels answered prayers?

In my family, we had a Quaker and a snake shaker,
a deal breaker and a no-more-dancing, parties maker

Vacation bible school, everyone gets dipped
in a dirty old tub,
my turn next, and they dunk me deep
in water made from spit of the saved

I felt that icky holy fluid backing up
in my throat and worried I might die
the prize is a little prayer and a child-sized bible
I want that miniature book

They say you must ask Jesus into your heart, but will he fit
I wonder, about a tiny Christ wedged beneath my ribs

Don't you want to be born again and cleansed of all your sins
how does it work - how will I know?
Got married in a church to please my nana
in the greater scheme of things, it made me happy too

she believed our love was sanctified - we were just young
and terrified of growing up and getting old and being alone

Hypocrisy through tithing lodges firmly in my gullet like a trout's bone
twelve months wed – the deacon called me to extort
we require additional payment for the grace of which you've been bestowed
NO! I yell, I paid my way, and my dues; you get no more from me

The next thing I recall, a baby, so small and sweet, cradled in my hands
you must bring that child to the lord – even strangers had opinions
I will not make her go until I find a place where I can
truly feel the love of something greater than myself
neighbors felt duty-bound to tell my precious bird that hell awaited
she sobbed, so confused, and I wept in fury thinking of those "good" Christians

Thirty-one years or more have gone, and I still believe in love
it was written in the stars, transcending all

And it doesn't cost a dime
God only knows.

Snowshoe Springs

My earliest memories,
I am aged two
sneaking into bed
with my big sister for a snuggle
I grasp my teddy bear
by his battered old leg and
squeeze him close
so he is protected
between her and me
once I've settled down,
my mind starts to wander
and soon, my body will follow

So I leave Percy Bear behind
and make my way
carefully
down the steep stairs on my butt
and slam (quietly) the front door of the cabin
in nothing but my wet diaper
that smells of detergent and pee

I scamper barefoot
through the fairy fern fields
that I have claimed
as magic and mine
and hear my Gramps
knock on the window
in smiling acknowledgment
he sees me - I am safe - he watches me - I am free

I spy
as squirrels and blue jays screech and holler
over cracked nuts and cantaloupe rinds

the day is already hot and sticky
with spiders and beetles
and some creatures
making an electric buzzing sound
my front forest renders me beautifully invisible
to all humans save for one

For a moment, there is only
the sound of my breathing
synchronized with nature
and all that surrounds me
then I hear the dear old man
in his faded, red long johns and a grey felt hat
as he crashes 'round the kitchen
his love language
is bacon grease, cussing, dirt, flapjacks, and me
I am his love language, and he is mine.

What Would the Neighbors Say

You mustn't brag
About yourself
Or call attention
To what you've got
Never speak
It's very private
Our secrets, you understand
We don't talk about it
Because it isn't very nice
So please, don't tell them
Anything controversial
Or it will be up and down the block
By the time we've finished dinner
A careless word or two
Is big news tomorrow
You know they only
Want to gossip
It's what they do
And we don't want
Them to guess
What our family life
Is really like
Honestly, girl
Must you tell everything you know
What would the neighbors say?

Red Motorcycle

Daddy was desperate
And needed to feel the open road
We bonded real strange over an old TV show
Starring Charles Bronson
All I remember is
We both loved it
I got to watch at night after I'd put on my pajamas
And once I started dreaming
Nothing would be good enough until I was allowed
On the back of that red motorcycle

Daddy was desperate
For a '69 XLH 900cc
Harley Davidson Sportster
Too rich for my family
What he had was a crappy little red Honda
He rode that bike to work with pride
Carried his grey lunch box
On its back, but never me
Maybe when you're five
He said, thinking surely I'd forget
But I watched that show and tried to learn
Anything to give me currency with him

Daddy was desperate
And we headed to the mountains
In a place with winding roads
To ride his red motorcycle
Please can I go, can I go
Take her, Dave — She won't be quiet until you do
No helmet, can you imagine? But safe enough
He looked at me and searched for flaws
Red bandana, Levi's, Old sweater, ratty Keds

He gave a great sigh — I guess we'll be okay
Come on, let's go

Daddy was desperate
This time, it isn't a grey lunch box; it's me
On the back of that red motorcycle
For safety's sake, you better hold on
I'm allowed to wrap my arms
Around his waist and lay my cheek against his back
I guess he'd do near anything to ride that bike
And my skin is covered with goosebumps
From the thrill of turns and straight-aways
And feeling loved, even if it was just one ride
Tears of unexpected origin streaked
The dirt on my little girl face
I tried to keep my mouth shut, so I didn't
Make a noise or swallow bugs

Daddy was desperate
For me to pay attention and not cause trouble
Although I worried I'd make mistakes, I still felt divine
Maybe if he knew how much I liked it
He'd stop, but I wasn't gonna tell
Holding on for safety's sake
Never knew quite if he loved me
My one and only shot to ride
On his red motorcycle.

Rain Always Brings You Back

Rain pounds on my roof
Suddenly, the you who I used to be is here
Kindergarten— walking alone to school
Splashing puddles, stomping, laughing
Wet pavement smell
Red rain slicker, shoes stuffed in boots
Bubble umbrella, metal lunchbox
Safe for daydreaming and strange freedoms
Rain always brings you back

A spaceship, a submarine, an arctic tundra
Pretending you've run away—you're so brave, Johnny Shiloh
Leaves swirl in gutters
Cross the big street, and forget to watch for cars
Splash of brown water, shushing, and a screech, horn blasting
Jump back into your body, back to now
Yelling man, shaking fists, angry scolding
Heart stops!
Rain always brings you back

Run the rest of the way to school
Kindergarten classroom, Good morning, children
Cloakroom full of sweaty boots and coats
Smell of mildew, unidentified darkness
Look in the mirror, and my eyes stare back
Hello, you
Braids askew, cheeks red
Fever-bright gaze, smile missing teeth
Rain always brings you back.

Ancestors

Eulogy

I imagine they're all together
And they can choose
Any version of themselves
From their wildest dreams

I like to think
Of the conversations
How welcoming they are
When a family member
Crosses over
How grateful that person is
To be with their loved ones again
To understand that someone
Who cared deeply for them
Was still watching out

I think about my mom and her brother
And their father—who left too soon
All the things they missed
How extraordinary it would be
If they had a chance
To start over

And all generations
Drawn into the circle of ancestors
Awaiting embrace
Not to rest peacefully
But to learn, and play, and love

Imagine them gathered
For stories and songs
I like to ponder
This other-world

All hurts settled
United in love
For the family
Rising above disputes
Squabbles
That plagued earthly bodies

How would it be for Abby
To speak with Abijah
And for the two of them
To finally
Mend fences
For Fred and Ralph
To find their
Brotherhood
And love they once shared
If Fred could speak
With his children and wife
And forgive

We speak of the afterlife
And perchance
The possibility
To do things over
In another lifetime
Better than the last.

Unwilling Subjects

Their wagons are circled
Once again, the first cousins
Huddled together to take refuge
From too little and too late
And humblest regrets
The underlying evasions
Are understandable
They pass the baton
From each to the other
Until we end at the beginning
As it was and ever shall be
With nothing resolved, settled, recorded
I love them deeply
Their loyalty and steadfastness
Even as they frustrate my efforts
With the vague promise
Of vast and untapped knowledge
And thwart my progress
While employing
Their tricks and genteel manners
Our unknown future
Preys upon me
And my constant awareness
Of time and its short supply
Please don't let me linger
Until there is nothing left to relay
And no one left to translate
Your Morse code messages
Allow me, if you will
To play archive to life's revelry
I'm begging you, cousins
Let me bear witness
To story and sorrow

Set the task
I'll provide the pen and ink
We are perfectly imperfect
There will be pain.

California Cowboys

Cowboys and best friends
Different as could be
Ranch hands, poets
Cattle drivers, hard drinkers

There was Old Wicked Tom
With his longwinded name
And shy Dayton Newell
Kinder than the day was long

Each night, bunkhouse supper
Five card stud, cheap whiskey
Then came the poems
Recitation, more booze

Whether Service or Poe
Wordsworth or Longfellow
Tired eyes, blurry and drooped
These men didn't care

Story poems - mystery and death,
Chances taken, warnings ignored -
Moiling Gold, they say
Recite then drink; drink then recite

Then came the day
They took to the trail
Time for them to ride
Dayton and Tom, side by side

Trail bosses, Poets, Drunks
Herding beeves for pay
Klamath Falls to Nevada City

288 miles, as the crow flies

Standard trail bill-o-fare
Hard Biscuits, beans, jerky, and coffee
Them, plumb out of booze
You can bet, after long hours worked

And stretched in never-ending hunger
It would try the most patient of men
With appetites so powerful
But worst was a thirst for the bottle

That's when the squabbling began
Tom stomped and trembled to walk on
Left Dayton out to dry
Bereft, hungry, and afraid

With friend and campfire in the distance
Old Tom hatched a plan
He was getting some grub
By hook or by crook

He spied a lone cabin
Empty yet full of things needed
If there was stealing to be done
That's where Wicked came in

Many and many times, all alone
Dayton sat there feeling guilty
On an old burned-out log
Bemoaning his own sorry fate

Then a rustling of bushes
Scared him near half to death
Ready to fight, he feared the worst
Then out popped friend Wicked Tom

Pulled a fresh chicken killed

From under his filthy coat
Then gutted and plucked it
Neat as you please

He skewered the heavenly bird
Cooked over hot coals
They ate fast and greasy
Like ravenous fiends

Dayton took a pull from
The newly filched bottle
Asked his friend
Where'd ya get that chicken

Shut up, eat, and give me a sip
They shared the booze
Harsh words in the past
Picked their teeth, rubbed their bellies

Dayton, old friend, no poetry tonight
I'm plumb-tuckered out
Then Wicked Tom rolled over, exhausted
And snored his way into dreams.

Children at a Birthday Party

Heartache and optimism
Move in cadence
I visit the same photo
To get a glimpse of the past
I am a time traveler -
Some belong to me
Complex and beautiful and spiraling
I try to puzzle the pieces

Children shine like new pennies
In their Sunday best
Seven clasp hands
In the cold and damp
The three on the end are family
Once upon a time,
Fast friends and playmates
Someday, they'll be together again

The tall girl in the old double-breasted coat
She stands with back straight
And her arms outstretched
Head tilted
Skyward and eyes closed
Forever a day-dreamer
Until her very end

Dark-haired boy -
Defiance steals his smile
Camera captures
Shy and a touch of trouble
He bears sadness
Forever frozen in time
Perhaps he has seen

Too much of what a child
Should not see
He is older brother and champion
Of the little red-haired girl

Her five-year-old delight is easy
Laughter,
Denial of any misfortune
Waiting just around the next bend
And wears her happiness
Like a cape of invisibility
This girl will wander the world
Yearning for safety and security
She holds my heart and soul
In the palm of her little left hand.

Walking on the Kingsbury Grade

Let me tell you about my adventure
Years ago when I was just a boy

Running beeves for winter grazing
Trail was rough, horseback a chore
It was Dad, my best friend Cousin Charlie, and me
Started from the home ranch - up north to Sis-ki-you
'Round the hard way to Knights Ferry
Then up again, Lake Tahoe, South

You really get to know a person on such a trip
When food is scarce, and work is hard
And bathing not at the top of the list

All we had to do was drop those cows in Minden,
And make it home for Christmas
One reason and another, the old truck wouldn't start
Crack of dawn, old boots on, walkin' home, time to go
Quit your bellyachin', boys, time to say goodbye
Set out on Route 19 to tramp those dirty miles
Dad rushed a hasty prayer, saints protect us travelers

Walkin' on the Kingsbury Grade
Along came a man in a 41 Chevy with a smile and a tip of his hat
You boys need a lift? Buddy you can bet we said yes.
Not walkin' on the Kingsbury Grade

Our man was a salesman, his car was a coupe and that suited us just fine
Milton was grateful, flat busted broke, we figured he had the time
He had a tank of gas and our fine company, those roads could give such a fright
Destination Frisco, just a little further, and he'd get us home

In we jumped, threw it into gear, and howdy what a ride
Speeding 'round the curves - brakes squealing somethin' fierce
Moving real fast, going good, then it got faster
Turns so tight I was sure we were gonna die

Did everything he could to keep us alive
Sweatin' in the backseat when he found an uphill rise
Thanks to St. Chris, we came screeching to a halt
Tumbled out wildly we thanked our lucky stars
Descent into o-bli-vi-on, thwarted at cliff's edge
By a tiny pine tree, growing from a rock the size of your head

You can keep your horses, and these damn modern cars
Lord, get us off of the Kingsbury Grade

Dedicated to my beloved cousins, R. J. W. and Charlie B.

Grief Wears Many Faces

I Want You to Know

If I know you, will I love you
The answer is yes

You told me everything, or
At least what you were able
Which turned out to be not much
You showed me the beauty of imperfection
On our journey, in this world, at this time
The answer is yes, I do love you.

We filled in life's details - found strange, hazy snapshots
Recollections of faces we didn't know
We had our secrets; we kept them close
From one another, and all we chose
The answer is yes, I do love you.

I asked questions. I asked so many
No matter the number, there were always more
I searched for truth. I was the psychic
I prayed I was mostly right or at least not mostly wrong
The answer is yes, I do love you.

My mind jumps from past to future
I can never quite catch up with your laughter or sadness
My fondest wish for you is peace
And that you realize you were good enough
The answer is yes, I do love you.

Here are my stories, my dreams, my poems
They are for you and about you—how you gave us all you had
A life crafted to keep us from harm and worry, to no avail
There can be no good without the bad
The answer is still yes, I do love you.

Familiar

Do you know me
It sticks in my throat
Truth is always
One step away
My fear's from the past

Who am I
Unwelcomed questions
Bitter knowledge
And softness that moves in the night
Stealing surety, vitality, history

Do I know you
Frail and watery blue eyes
A pale replacement
For laughter and Sunday dinners
Fear and grasping hands
Trying to hold on to
One more moment, please
Must find clarity
We left it in the trunk of the car
Stare in confusion

Where did I go
Thoughts meander
Rote and meaningless
My nana didn't recognize
Me at my own wedding
It was robbery
Life and unfairness
Unyielding motion
Brink of madness

Do I look familiar?

Orange Geraniums

Orange Geraniums in our front yard
Were your favorite color and my most dreaded hue
That particular scent
Earthy, grassy, citrusy
Perfect for generations of snail colonies
Especially after a good soaking rain
Orange Geraniums in our front yard
Until they weren't
One day they vanished abruptly
I don't know why
But I know you loved them
And that they were your favorites
It should have been enough for me
You know I never liked them
I found them to be too bold, overly sentimental, and old fashioned

The other day at the nursery
Imagine my surprise
To find amongst the rows
Of pinks, reds, whites, purples
One orange geranium
Basking in the late autumn sunshine
Waiting with great expectation
My eyes filled with tears
I said hello to you
And took that plant home
I placed her lovingly,
On my front porch
Where every time I see her bloom
I'll see you, too.

Silence

I can no longer
conjure how it felt
to hear your voice
perhaps brief moments
when I catch a trace
and then
it is disappeared
dispersed out to the
universe
sounds become
an empty cupboard
filled with nothing
there is a hole where
your singing occupied
a space just so
and another where vibrations
of your crying used to
fit just here under my heart
places where harsh words
were in residence
or where the joyous syllables flowed
and what of the spaces
where all the words we
should have said were placed
a walk into an empty room
will often let me hear you
say my name
in that irritating way
little snippets
of conversation filter through
but it is never enough
never enough for me
unique to you and now silent.

Two Years, Seven Months, Two Days

Today I am awash in memories
I think about you singing
While doing the dishes
Led Zeppelin songs
And I suppose we're never too old
Been a long time since I rock and rolled
Two years, seven months, two days

Yesterday, I thought about you
Twisting my long hair up in rag curls
And I'd wake up in the morning
With my hair tangled in the curlicues of my headboard
Two years, seven months, two days

Once you told me a story how you were sick
When you were a little girl - diphtheria they said
On the ceiling, in the corner of the bedroom
You saw a vision of the Virgin Mary
No money to be had for medicine or doctors
Only dandelion greens from the garden
Prepared by our women for generations
And brewed into a healing tea
I try to imagine how it would feel
To be the little girl saved by Jesus' mama and greens
Two years, seven months, two days

Someday maybe I'll lose my mind
Until then, I write my remembrances faithfully
I don't want to forget a minute, Mama
All the details will be saved
And you'll never be lost
Two years, seven months, two days

I dream, I wish, I pine
I long to share my secrets with you
And I believe you hear me
Isn't it strange how
I still try to protect you
From the bad stuff
But most times, I can laugh when I think of you
Except on days when I want to ask you about this and that
Except on days I desperately want to hear your voice
Except on days I'd give anything to feel your embrace
Two years, seven months, two days

I long for proximity
A word that could never equal my yearning
At least
In the universe and in forever and in my dreams
You and I are in close proximity.

Lost Years

our strides chew the earth
plowing forward
with purposeful movement

our destination is *the* destination
greater than or equal to the whole (me 56, you 64)

lou reed, rock and roll animal
- frightening me,
drawing me in,
helplessly appealing
- scratchy speakers and
dirty
(phonographic)
needles

-- control

life is like one of those documentaries where you can't seem to stop
watching
even with fingers pressed against your eyes
and your racing, foolish heart in your
throat

something in that thrilling agony of being chosen - noticed
it came on the heels of motherly admonishment
and arrived with emotional furor
the sweet anxiety of being selected for adventure

piling into the backseat with all your friends (you 16, me 8)
and knowing this was not the assignment,
I was not part of the caper,
but secretly elated to be included,

terrified by the prospect of losing control
the breath of resentment as it fogs your glasses

I pressed my face tight against a smeared window - (inhale)
and watched the colors as they ran down the car door in the rain
the deepening twilight's mist
and the scent of weed—intoxicating,
sharp, and specific - (exhale)

Salvador Dali lived until the year 1989 but before that happened
we made a special trip - for *Lincoln in Dalivision* -
and pixilation before it became a common thing (1978)
in a small space somewhere
in one of those neighborhoods where galleries
co-exist with matter and time
yes, I saw this work and have only now found the memory of it
as being rather sweet and soft
and will be forever imprinted in my mind
as is the artist,
as is the day,
as are you,
as am I

I remember the joy I felt when art provided context for us

We found etchings of Charles Bragg, an American artist
I was charmed by his playfulness, sarcasm, grainy darkness,
I loved the absurdity
it appealed to my teenage psyche

we are our exploration -
everywhere and every when
you pulled me into your whirlwind

there is a cracking open of my scull (soul)
and possibilities crash like ocean waves
from my eyes and ears and mouth and nose -

surprise Spanish guitar
and a promise of practice I eventually would come to loathe -
we walked miles on that overcast day
and it felt perfectly fine to be part of something
even if I didn't know what the hell
that something was
and suddenly
we'd traveled far
and all the particles in the universe
bumped up against other bits
of space gunk and memory -
all must change or die (you 20, me 12)

stoned revelry in a hooptie fastback
on a winding country road
in the middle of bedroom communities
and 10-second rural feelings slipped by too fast
I was part of the thing, and it was too late to forget
but it begged for promise of clarity
always on the outside looking in

-- release

and now it's all
beautiful random reflections
in our aviator sunglasses and rearview mirrors (me 57, you gone)

When I'm Done

Still catch myself thinking
I should call you
To relay messages
And greetings of my day
A fleeting moment passes
Before I realize
I can't do that anymore
And I feel the sadness
Of those thoughts
Weighing down upon me
Like a flat river rock
Pressing and squeezing
The air from my chest
The pages of your life
Have all been read
And someday, so will mine
Until then, I will wait
To be reunited once again.

Glorious Nature

Breathe

What do you need, sweet soul
where are you hurting
give your mind a rest
take a moment to replenish
that which the world drains from you
be loving, be gentle
with yourself

Dirt under your nails
scrape at the soil
work the earth
plant for your sustenance
watch tender spouts find
strength and courage
to be kissed by the sun

Be in savasana
melt into mother earth
hear soft chanting of breath
imbued with devotion
as your body and heart
are cradled in comfort
peace descend upon you

Imagine taking flight
as the red-tail hawk
air currents love you
lift and dip
feathers ruffle
slightest movement
tracked by your eye

Count three, hold
mantra meditation
secret incantation
interior journey
visualize a pathway
be love in this moment
count three, expel

Crown - divinity
third eye - intuition
throat - blessed voice
heart - accept love
solar plexus - power within
sacral - pleasure
root - belonging

Breathe and be.

Dragonfly Season

Sweet summer air
Filled with magical creatures
They flit about here and there
Always graceful
How lonely I'd be
Without their ancient cerulean, emerald, and amber selves
Bright early morning speaks drowsily
Of soaring temperatures
Stinging heat and thickly blanketed air
I yawn and stumble outside
And stretch sleepily
Awakened by nature
My sweet dog companion, watches my every move
He sits as close to me as he can
Then closer still
Warmth radiates from his little body
And soft rivulets of sweat
Trace wet tracks down my back
Iced coffee quenches momentary thirst
We watch, in silent fascination, all we can spy
Beings that dart and crawl and scamper
Hummingbirds, Lizards, Bees
Grey Squirrel pokes his head above the deck
Temporarily thwarted by our presence
He stamps a hind leg
Shows his great displeasure
We keep him from his breakfast
A young rooster practices
His very own cock-a-doodle-do
At the little farm
On the other side of my hill
Gentle horse asks for his oats
Persnickety goldfinches delight

As they gossip at the feeder
Spilling as much as they consume
Mourning Doves light
On the metal dish for their morning bath
- they've paused their journey to partake
Of a delicate sip and dip the tip of their wing
In shallow water, warming in the sun
The dragonflies are more spectacular this year
Than I can ever recollect
And the rest of the world is held at bay
A few
Minutes
More.

Lavender and Bees

Come harvest, they said
at the Lavender farm
if they love you
the bees leave you alone

Scent and sound
fill my head
I'd be lying
if I didn't say it
makes me wary
my fear of the sting

I cannot ignore
tiny harbingers
of life and bloom

I went freely amongst rows
of soft purples and pinks
and the little flying dears
did not harm me

They sidled up to me
as I carefully pruned
always leaving more
than I took

The sounds of buzzing
hypnotic and sweet
pure magic as they drank
their lavender tea

You have not lived until
you've seen thousands

of bee butts drunk
quite tipsy, they were
not bothered
in the least, with
human intrusion

I always include
different varieties of
lavender in my garden
a delicious repast should
the bees ever come for tea.

A Realization of Spiders

When did I stop watching
As spiders spun their webs
As a child, I had the pure and uncanny
Ability to look at something
For a split second
And gather every bit of information available
Oh! There is a web
Look how it stretches from
The fencepost, to the rosebush, to the water spigot
How long did it take her to make
That stained glass window
Of design and dew and the wing of an old fly
How magical her spider geometry
And does she have babies
Somewhere in a protected little sack
Waiting to be born
And how long to rebuild
If I brush through it
Accidentally
With my hands, or hair, or shoulder
I might not even notice until later
When I realized that sticky silken stuff
Trailing from me
A sad reminder that I'd disturbed
Her life's work
I was already fascinated by her care and industry
And then I read, *Charlotte's Web*
Where the author anthropomorphized
His characters so perfectly
And made me love spiders even more

Now that I'm a grown-up
I hardly ever think about spiders

Unless they get in my way and need to be removed
I don't remember the last time
I daydreamed over a beautiful web
And that seems sad and small
I hope I still remember how to find them.

Bee Hives

Such lovely sticky
honey to be had
just down the road

a few miles west
so many hives
and I know

the almonds
cherries and apples
blackberries

make the honey
even sweeter
brilliant nature

delicate chambers
amber light
treasures

he mourns
as he drives through
and hears the splat

of many bees
meeting death
on his windshield

I have to love
a man who
gets misty

about those bees
he wants to warn
the farmers

and make them
move the hives
so they'll be safe

babe, they're
there for reasons
part of the plan

but it is the hill
my man stands upon
hive attrition.

Nesting Box

On the highway home, along fence lines
Bluebird nesting boxes
Are dotted
You noticed them
Of course, you noticed

You told me about them - those tidbits
Wide-eyed joy, your avid interest
Like a squirrel or a toddler or just your
Unbridled enthusiasm
For hidden and obscure and a bit odd

So. Nesting boxes are not
Birdhouses or cages. They function
And line the roadway
We wondered could we have one
Are we clever enough for those birds

There's something not quite
Of-this-world about bluebirds
Brilliant, startling, bold
And mama weeps over babies
Are you bluebird graced

Don't pass us by without a glance
Build a home, a box, for safe
On the hill, we waited
And waited - while our hopes
Came dashed and dejected

Then one late spring day
Two years in the future
Electric blue flashes - oh, they dart

No leisurely stroll, our bluebirds
They are speed and economy

Manzanita shrubs are alight
Something tasty for supper
Was it the special freeze-dried worms
Our hillside menu was judged adequate
And they sing a little

It's not that we have bluebirds, mind you
More they visit - when they're up to it
We gasp when we see our hillside
Turn most magical of colors
Don't be sad.

This poem is dedicated to the memory of Charles Bukowski and his poem Bluebird.

Damselfly

Delicate double-wings
Hovering a moment
On the little lake
Amongst cattails and rushes
I looked into her eyes
Wondering how I must appear
Jerky movements
Slow
Not a ballerina
I was loud and needed a nap
But instead
I was fishing in my own world
Little red plastic pole and bobber
And I loved watching anything
That moved or flew or crept or hid
Pollywogs fascinated
Butterflies entranced
But Damselfly
She was like a tiny steed
I imagined
Riding triumphantly on her back
A softly woven
Saddle and reins of golden thread
Something for me
To hold on to
Not to be used for control
She wore an iridescent toque
Reserved for royalty
I wielded the trusty sword in my scabbard
And we flew
Over hills and meadows and streams.

Cracked Open

Find me
please
my depths
these
crystal bridges
jagged facets
mirrored and
reflective rooms
the geode
must be opened
to be understood
crack me open.

Flow

Such grace, your headwaters
Lake Tear of the Clouds
Source of sweet clarity
Life-giving mystery
Rise from infancy
Travel more than 300 miles
Never to return home
Growing, twisting, turbulent
Passive, calm, whitewaters
Rushing currents
Warm pools, tender dips
Your shape and the places you chose
To twist and curve
Nothing short of alchemy
How deep, how shallow
How placid, how rough
Old magic
Goddesses and gods
Dwelling within you
Splashing, dancing, crying
Sleeping, birthing
Continuous cycle
You flow two ways
And just as if it's the end
Of a glorious night
You can't say goodbye to love
Your waters mingle and taste
Just at the mouth
Playfully, gently, purposefully
Where fresh becomes brackish, then salty
And home is an ocean
At World's End
You are Mahicantuck.

Smoke Cherry

Pretty little thing
You won't last long
When winter's gone
Smoke cherry

Intoxicating scent
You hurt my heart so bad, darlin'
And money's all been spent
Smoke cherry

You make it hard to say goodbye
I wish you'd make it easy, baby
Gotta stop and wonder why
Smoke cherry

Your delicate blooms are fallen
And spring just in the air
Burgundy leaves, I still believe
Smoke cherry.

Conversations with Gravity

There's something I want you to see
boulders and rocks
obscured by all the wildflowers

> *you mean the poppies and lupines*

yes, those
scramble on your belly, careful, careful
keep your wits about you and move
slow, not so fast, not so fast!

> *I see, but what am I looking for*
> *oh, the river, the river!*
> *it's moving so swiftly*

I wish we could get to that spot
right down there, but it's too far and too steep
when I looked down I feel vertigo
do you feel it too

> *no, and I don't mind it at all*
> *it's so peaceful here, peaceful here*
> *this spot is miraculous*
> *I could spend a million years just so and with you*

well, it makes me dizzy, don't look down, don't look down

> *how can I see anything if I don't look down*
> *I'll be okay. Don't worry*

I want to believe
but there's something about this exact spot
these native plants and scree that makes me want to lean

a little further forward and tip just beyond the edge
this place is purely magical and I feel a lack of control

> *it almost seems as though gravity has been suspended*
> *and the rocks want us for their own*

don't look down, don't look down!

Filled with Joy

There's an indent in the slab of granite
On the river
In the mountains
Near my home
A hole
Not natural but never out of place
Intentionally created
For blessed use
And when I came upon it
Thousands of years
Opened in my mind
And I saw
Beautiful caretakers of the land
Sit and work in the sunlight
Diligent women of an ancient culture
Worked relentlessly
At this boulder's perfect structure
Bald eagles flew overhead
Fish jumped in clear waters
They came day after day
Wore away at it
Intentionally, carefully
Strength of purpose
Until finally, it was
Right size and shape and depth
For cupping water
For holding grain
For making sustenance
Willfully exacting domination
Over nature but in such a kind way
That the forces of the universe
Could only smile and watch
As its creations created

What they most needed
And the grandmothers and granddaughters sat side by side
Filled
With
Joy.

Lightning Rod

I'm a city girl
living in a rural community
on the edge of great forests
near high country where weather
during wildfire season, is paid close attention
one summer night
when it was so damn hot
I could swear my eyelids were sweating
so I took a little drive
to my favorite lake
a little more than 30 miles up the road
trying to find sweet relief
I sat on a bench and contemplated
the universe
bald eagles
tourists
and how I wasn't those things
but could relate to them in my own way
a thunder and lightning storm broke
no rain, at least not yet
dry lighting is dangerous
but still, I watched transfixed
by the power and glory of nature
the violence and utter disregard
for me and my silly soul
I laughed how, in the middle of high season
I was the only one left at the shore
watching little anchored sailboats bob on the water
getting ready for the storm
bald eagles moved on
tourists gone home
universe remained
there I sat, a lightning rod, on a bench
at a lake in the woods.

Run Free

We, on the edge of wilderness
Live in self-imposed
Proximal confines
And trade the air we breathe
For creature comforts
Head now toward sunrise
Where the body shivers
And a popping shift in senses
From greed to gratitude
Is the sound of shedding
Metaphorical clothing
Feel whispered omens
Go further backcountry
Where the light will change
The horizon broadens
Constellations nearly touch
The tip of a nose
Until we are naked
Under stars and moon
Breath comes deep and sharp
Scented by snow, pine, and dirt
Cold, cold, and clean
Alone and awake
Skin tingles
Searching
For warmth from our core
Steam and vapor rise
Desperate to find river's edge
Free to run
To escape the coil.

Stormy Skies

I love a stormy sky
In the morning
How the air
Smells of quickness
When wind howls
And rain on the roof
Wakes me
I love those dark clouds
Hanging so low
Sure I can reach up and grab them
I love watching lightning strike
Like detonating fireworks
I love a green glow
Now sizzling purple
Hot white
Golden blaze
The equation of thunder
I love counting how close
With Mississippi's
I wait breathlessly
Wondering if the science is right
I love sitting on the edge of the lake
And imagining
Magic shows in the dark
Of giants and gods walking
Heavy-footed
Through strange mountains.

The Element of Water

This morning I dreamed
I was promised renewal
At water's edge
No written contract but simply a legitimacy
To be invited - to a test of boundaries
I skipped quickly
While skimming rocks in the surf
And avoided greenish, yellowish foam
Which hid sharp objects and jellies
I noticed that here on the shore of the Pacific
Even the ugly things have great beauty
Perhaps I would be as welcomed
As small pieces of driftwood
Some smooth and sensual
Some rough and unfinished
How bereft I'd be to never know
The pleasures of the great salty tides
To never turn cartwheels
In the shallows until
I dropped dizzy and elated
Into the creeping waves
When the sun was at its zenith
I sat and meditated for a while
Burning my lips and nose and cheeks
On that ever-present reflection
That vast mirror
Mark the edges
Of what was and what was not
I never could tell you
All of the things that moved
Through my mind during those sessions
Except it felt like being reborn
In those rough, liquid, languid moments

I belonged in the society of hermit crabs
And sea kelp ripped from its underwater forest
By the push and force of the brine
And shells with iridescent glamour
A welcome snack
In the greedy beak of a persistent gull
I have seen tide pools that reminded me
Of ancient caches of buried treasure
A distant question rises -
When does the pebble become the sand
And why are the glinting pieces
So elusive and uniform
And the larger pieces so singular
Please let me come back to this place
Where the water renews my spirit.

First Time

They sprouted
Grew under the soil
Pushed up
Into the morning
Photosynthesis
Pretty alchemy
Rain and sunlight
And, I'm convinced
My chants of "GROW"
Another day, more progress
I watched closely
Kept those dastardly earwigs
From chewing your leaves
Placed netting all round
To keep out the squirrels and deer
I companion-planted
Zinnias and Marigolds
To thwart other wayward pests
Until beyond my wildest dreams
One morning late in June
I spied a remarkable thing
And then another
Oh, my delight
In this patch, I'd so lovingly tended
There they were
Zucchinis and cucumbers
Sweet peas and radishes
Tomatoes and Potatoes.

Brittle

I can see I've spent
just enough time
digging through my garden
happy plants but
I look like a farmer
not a gentlewoman
ragged, black at the cuticles
brittle fingernails
my hands not soft
I am industrious
and unafraid
of a little
dirt.

Where I Feel Most Alive

Water sparkles
Like diamonds in sun
Thunder crashes
Lightning dances
Wind in trees
Whispers ancient secrets
Snow flowers push
Winter-hardened earth
Crow circles, caws
Spies a shiny thing
Rainbow trout thrive
Bask in the riverbed
Air is clean and sharp and bold
Tar scent of mountain misery
Travels on the breeze
Stones and boulders and pebbles
They know their hierarchy
Ground squirrels
Stomp and click and cavort
My loneliness
Escapes on a sigh
I am pure delight
In this place
I will only ever be
A visitor
Where I feel most alive.

Wild Fire

My flames
Lick
Trees and underbrush
I devour all in my path
Fuel for my insatiable thirst
Burn, incinerate
Bonfires dance and spark
Smoke, joy rises
Draft creates hot winds
Whirling towers
Flames and ash
Add water
My steam will scorch
Leaving nothing but yesterday's relics
Tiny flare
Puff of air
And I'm back- razing the earth
I seek what you protect
My pyre unstoppable
Time and circumstance
Flash of light - rotten limb cracks
Race to envelop and consume
All eyes watch as I become
Fully involved and engaged.

There is no Light without Darkness

Barest Concessions

We know
these truths
in our hearts and minds

a human being
can have a life
surrounded by others
and feel absolutely
adrift and un-tethered
so lonely

you begin to fear you'll fade from existence
like you might die from the suffocation
of emptiness

to live
to be alive is pain
and pain goes away after we die
and then...

you can be in a room
with another person
and be utterly alone
no matter how you try
there are no words
of comfort
there are no soft touches
no gentle kisses
no warm embraces
it is just you and them
for eternity
unfulfilled passion
empty words

not brave confessions or barest concessions
worn-out phrases

you might feel all alone
but we're not supposed to be alone.

Elevator

Tying a Windsor knot
- that's me in the mirror
I barely recognize the woman I am
Crowded together
Strangers and random uncivilized armpits
My color palette today
- always grey, always black
The metal box fills
Seven, please
14
Just push 25
Would you?
Old and new collide
- misery mixed with mercy
Mercury retrograde and cough drops
A cloying scent assaults
- there ought to be a law
Estee Lauder's youth dew
Blended carefully
Cigarettes, tuna noodle casserole, and cheap gin
Bring it home
Hollow desperation
A smug expression
One day bleeds into a thousand
Meet up at the Kerry House
Panic, bowels gone to water
Left-over nausea
Nearly to the top
Soon the leftovers overflow
Today's mental see-saw
- good enough, not good enough
10 hours later
- back in the box

Push the button
Plummet to the basement
Arrive with a bone-rattling crash.
Dust it off
Look familiar
Never mind, you
Go home, see the husband
Make love, hide your angst, bite your tongue
Thrash in bed
Dream of death
Sweat clear through to the mattress
The radiation of the morning sun
Scorches your eyelids
Do it all again.

When It Comes to You

Forgive and forget
Love and behave
No one ever wants to see
The boat-rocker
There have been times when
I'm able to forget that you could be
Monstrous and overpowering
Frighteningly violent
Brilliant and calculating
I lie to myself
Do not upset the status quo
Pretend my life was ideal
and
I was a good, safe girl
I think about the things
you did and tried to do
I'm sorry you were
tortured, misunderstood
I know life was unfair
I remember how it went down
A shocking disparity
Between what was real
and
What was seen from the outside
The casual and secret violence
Violation must only be a dream
When I was told
My job was to be brave
No congratulations
Shut up
Stop telling our secrets
You live in the past
My truth

I will not be afraid
I open my mind
I take a deep breath
You cannot define me
When it comes to you.

Nothing

I prayed I would be
Transformed
Into some bright star
In your heavens
The harder I tried
The further from me you drifted
The more I wanted you to notice me
Admire me
The less you acknowledged
My existence
Why do I always love the ones
Who are unattainable
The ones who look upon me
With disdain and, eventually contempt
You were all of the things
I would cherish most.

In your universe, I meant nothing.

Overheard Conversation

He spoke with a smile, explaining his thoughts
When you get through this breakup with me
You're going to bloom
Like the flower, you were meant to be
This will be your proving ground
Making something good from something damaged
You'll be a more resilient woman

Fuck you, she said
I'm perfect as I am
A perfect flower, a perfect bloom
I'm already strong, so don't you placate me
The best thing to come out of this mess
Is the death of excuses
And your bad behavior.

After Las Vegas

I'm drowning today
falling and flailing
struggling to breathe
anguish and anxiety
lack of gravity
lack of promise
lack of faith

I witness our country
consequences of inconsequential
disenfranchised, marginalized, powerless
assaulted
as powerbrokers
spew and proclaim
they swear
by all that is holy

I swear to the saints
a thousand rounds
if I hear one more politician spout
their thoughts and prayers
How do you reconcile 61 dead
867 injured
I do not know
a fucking sound-bite
something meant to lend
love and support
reduced to a withered husk
and lack of sincerity has become a
rusty knife digging bullets
from festering wounds

I persist in my belief
insist all along
is love, is love, is love.

Dormant

I was sure
it was over
hadn't seen
you in years
got to a place
where I could
go weeks
without your
words and
voice and smell
and look
reminding me
fear
the nausea
the tightness
in my belly
lay dormant
a quiet rotten
kernel living
secret in my
memory
then someone
saw that you
had left this
world and all
of my hard
work came
crashing down
on me and my
well ordered
private life.

Heirlooms

Sometimes you get things
You should not have
And do not want

Connections to someone
No longer in my life

Then a tiny crack
In my armor
Or a window left open
Accidentally
And you are back
Exactly where you took up
Residence in my brain

I was sure it had all been
Purged, but now
Fetid air and nightmares
When I received the gifts
From your estate
I knew it was nothing
But a kind gesture
On behalf of your friends
But those things
Will never heal me
They hamper my recovery
How were they to know
I never told them
I intended to keep this secret
Because it hurts

Those gifts are still there
Breathing and waiting

And lie like
A last little swallow
Of poison in my bottle.

Judgment

If you insist on judging me
narrow-minded ignorance
will get you only so far
save up those excuses
for someone who cares
get out, get it over with
I don't speak to anyone
in particular, but I do call out
those who believe it is
acceptable to objectify
when I say you are dirty-minded
I don't mean this in a lascivious way
I mean, your words feel besmirched
I find them mean and petty and foul
stain-filled and irrelevant
to my goals, my plans, my intentions.

Mon Ami, Mon Amour

Early Morning Light

Where did I misplace
the rainbows
that magically appeared
each morning
in our bedroom
and sometimes
in afternoon
coming through
the front windows
I miss the lovely
camera obscura
of lace patterns
that danced in the breeze
how the shadows and light
created their own
pantomime of reality
those tiny miracles
of nature and luck.

My Favorite Place

Rotting papaya
rain-dampened soil and leaf mold
the earthy dark scent of sticky frangipani
cushions the song of a thousand birds
colors flash bright and give way
their hidden spaces in the trees
a yellow wing here, a red bit there
in my dream, I woke today next to you
warm and sweat-drenched
scents blended in this tropical climate
we stretch and giggle and run
to the lapping water's edge
sand squeaks, and toes sink in
the air off the ocean breathes its own symphony
and we slide into her wet warmth
as she embraces us in her salty goodness
we surface dive and immediately
spy a school of luminescent coronet fish
darting in tandem with our heartbeats
and come up for air
ecstatic with our discovery
we play and splash arms and legs entwined
until hunger overtakes
I loved you so back then in my favorite place.

Jolly Rancher

Roll it 'round your mouth
like a jolly rancher
get those glands behind
your jawbones working
salivating just by
the thought of it
craving the sweet, the salty, the sour
no baby, no,
just craving you.

Fnar

The first time you said it
I giggled and blushed
Surely someone who'd use this term
Must be filled with wit and clever rejoinder
And oh, sir, you certainly were
The second time you said it
I was captured by your cunning sparple
You wanted me here
You led me on a merry chase over there
Until I walked willingly into your trap
It was when you said wit woo
That I knew you'd want me too
It was charming as charming could be
Dare I say you are quixotic
As I collapse
Weakened by your blandishments
The third time it was uttered
You had me - your smile, your jest
Perfectly compliment
My strangely garrulous nature
Your teasing and banter
Make me weak in the knees
With your perfected persiflage
And all I can reply is
Ah, you
Fnar.

Heart of Desire

These possibilities leave me
nervous
excited
I long for something I never knew
Feeling myself blooming
Like sticky star Jasmine
Its aroma sends me into a dream, a reverie
A state of drowsy awareness
I gasp for breath as
My heart beats time to my arousal
And my body opens to your touch.

This Poem is a Secret

I
have
a secret
it is you and
your attention
and how you make
me feel alive and whole
perhaps for the first time in
forever your possession gives me
full autonomy to be anything I choose.

Broken

My love is an
oddly shaped
smile
a chip in a cup
saucer or tooth
I love those bits
that some
might throw
away
those broken
things many
try to ignore
I love how your flaws
match mine
and
do you think that
mine match yours
and perhaps you
might be broken, too.

Yearning

I spent today yearning
There's a hitch in my breath
And whispers in my heart
As I pine for your warmth
And pray for your scent
The sound of your voice
Is the music in our song
My love, I could write
A thousand lines
In praise of your skin
And never be able to express
How you bring me to my knees
With a single look.

Honey Mead

Pagan wedding
Honey mead
Under stars and moon
Dancing in darkness
Undeniable
With each other
Flowers in hair
Barefoot in grass
Sticky nectar
Kiss my neck
Honey mead
Come here you
Rock me gently
Gather me near
Well after midnight
Walking in moonlight
A secret place
Back in shadows
We were alone
We didn't care
Heady scents
No consequence
Howling coyotes
Owls hoot and screech
Music far off
Laughter and singing
Serenading
Honey mead
We find each other
Just us in the meadow
Damp grass clings
To bodies heated
In summer's sweat

We move together
A rhythm we set
Honey mead
Drip from me
Honey mead
I want you - I do.

Spark

I did not know, my love
That our fires would bank
And our ember's spark
Would reduce to a small puff of smoke
If only we could take great pains
And restore the flames with just a bit of oxygen
To find that now, as we both age
Trust and mercy must abound
And love's shape changes as we are sated
Often becoming something
We scarcely recognize
But fostered with both time and care
Opening our hearts
To more reverence and devotion
Than we could ever comprehend
Vastly different and yet the same, reflecting us
Each path converging one upon the others
Righteous love conquers all
The spark ignites the flame.

Navigating Bodies

Oceanic maps and ciphers
Desire and joy and passion
Shivers and delicious chills
While wind roses chart
Our speed and directions
Heat and movement
Breaths accelerate
Into the reflecting circle
Oh! celestial bodies measured
We move and embrace
Drawing closer than close
A blending, a melding
Spied by astrolabe
Like ships on the ocean
Undulating atop one set of waves
Crashing wildly down
To be raised by traverse board
Over hills and valleys of one another
Let me learn your body
Like the lines on my hands
So I may never forget
How you feel under my fingertips
By backstaff and by sextant
Please tell me you will learn mine
I will teach you what makes me gasp and sigh
And beg you my darling
To be an apt pupil and bring you delight
Slick sweat slips down the back of your neck
Runs down your spine with absolute bearing
Magnetized compass of touch
Your heady scent, your callused palms
The darkness and promise in your eyes
Your jaw, collarbones, and lips
Your lead lines, all so perfect, so beautiful.

Broken Hearted

They told me you'd
Been rushed to the hospital
No further information
Available at this time
Are you alive

Echoes grew louder
Until I cannot feel
My lips moving
Come immediately
I am compelled
Be alive. Be alive. Be alive

Beating like a drum
The beating of a heart
Shock tries to complete
A circuit from body to brain
Silly to imagine
I was in control
I did not know
If you were alive

To exist in the universe
One without the other
Seemed a cruel trick
As I moved east to west
Are you alive

I was terrified to ask
I was molasses
Every door adorned
Bright red valentines
Cardiac unit

Then I heard your soft voice
Hope blooms in my breast
And there you are
Pale and weakened since last
We saw each other this morning
You are alive

Hooked up, beeping machines
The one I've loved since 1980.

Forbidden Fruit

I could do
No more than taste
And once I had
I knew
I would never stop
Your sweetness
Ripe like cherries in summer
Your dangers
Ignite fire
Wherever your steps wander
My heart beats hard
And breaths come shallow
In your presence
Your words drip like
Honey from a hive
I was warned
Away more than once
From the peril
That is you
But still
I keep coming back for more.

House

Long, dark hallways
Too many doors
Too few closets
Drafts that chill
From basement to attic
Rattling windows
Mismatched door-jambs
Cracks in the ceiling
Greasy finger
Smudges on walls
Scuffed hardwood
Chipped tiles
Stained formica
Leaky faucets
Appliances gone
To wrack and ruin
We cry because
No matter what we do
This house will never be
Fixed or finished
And when we are fragile
Completely beyond our ken

Where we fight and love
And know as many
Inner thoughts
As one can understand
About another
Vulnerabilities out on display
Where we could easily tear
One another apart, but don't
Our fondest wishes
Kept safe and unexamined

Because it is ours and not theirs
Where secrets sleep safely
One look and a million thoughts
Jumble into the unsaid
Because we are imperfect
In this place, in this lifetime
We belong to one another
For better and worse
You are my home.

My Wish for You

I wish
And
You dream
Tranquil bridges
Colors
Light and sound
That strongly, strangely, stay
All within your grasp
Even as you wake
They lovingly
Watch over you
Those guardians
Just
At the edge of now.

It Breaks You

When someone intuits
what's deep in your heart
and it breaks you
before they open
their mouths to speak.

Proper

I want a taste
the smallest
little sample
let me, please

I am greedy
although I know
sharing is right
and proper

There is nothing
proper
about the way you
make me feel.

Sharp Edges

Grasp my world
by its sharp edges, darling
and pray for a thousand years more.

Tough Love

Let us be any way
We're meant
Hands on hips
Arm across shoulders
Our many complications
These lives together
Shared
Sharpened
Sweetened
Tangled messily
Painfully, joyously
I barely remember me before you
I'll never insist on easy
What worthwhile journey ever is.

Mojave

Damped skin reflected
by a waxing gibbous moon
distant songs play
as meteor showers
mirror in your eyes
it is our desert longing
coyotes howl from a far-off place
and tiny creatures skitter
over this harsh ground
scent of sage and nighttime sweat
a fragrant perfume
ferocious beats of our hearts
and blissful sacred sounds
echo through the Mojave
our kisses filled with longing
never to be quenched
limbs that twist and dance, entwined,
let us explore together
gratefully leave mundane behind
let the mind quiet as pleasure overtakes
I see your soft smile
your hungry expression
that tangled hair
and the planes of your hip
such muscular thighs
we pant and then quiet to listen
then you call to me again
all hardness and eloquence
let us lovers begin the dance
once again, Mojave.

See Me

Duality

My need is a living, breathing	My soul is that of an angel
greedy thing	most tender and delicate
stronger and more self-sustaining	stronger and more self-sustaining
than you could ever imagine	than you could ever imagine
I may tell you I'd like one, please-	I will give anything you need
one kiss, one minute, one chance	one kiss, one minute, one chance
while inside I beg	and you may ask
for more and more and more	for more and more and more
fill me 'til my cup runneth over	fill me 'til my cup runneth over
my need fears rationing	my soul radiates gladness
and being trapped in a desert	and abundance
of unquenchable thirst	the sweetest honey mead
it fears starvation	most precious sustenance
of the self and of love	for body, mind, and spirit
it waits patiently for me to break	I may break, but love and kindness
used and exhausted	shall follow me
it bides time until I	waiting for me to heal
crumble and weep	courageous and unbroken
my need tells me lies	my soul know the truth of me
that I'll never find grace	from the top of my consciousness
or be enough of the good things	to the bottom of my heart
and you will run a million miles	and you will run a million miles
in the opposite direction	to find me
because I am facetious	because I am yours
difficult, intractable	worthy, splendid
unworthy, despicable	deserving, engaging
and unpleasant.	and an utter delight.

You Were Born with Wings

When I was a girl,
I dreamed of flying
I'd just about get off the ground
when something would tug me back
I'd drop like a stone
and awaken, confused.

When I was a young woman,
I learned to fly at the end of a tether
with just enough rope to taste freedom
but not so much that I'd disappear from my life altogether
I'd be reeled in
feel the memory
and smile sadly, secretly about my gift.

When I was a woman,
I stopped wanting to fly
it was for someone else, not me
but deep inside, I ached
I lied to myself
then I stopped dreaming.

When I was an older woman,
I questioned my time on this earth
and my ideas
laughed with friends
and tried new things
then I woke up one morning
and realized that not only had I dreamed
but in that dream
I had flown.

Incantation

Do not let them scare you
rob you of your sleep
do not let them in
unless you want to let them in
let me comfort you
let me be the thing you need
let me put your fears to rest
lay your head upon my breast
there are ghosts and ghosts of dreams
dwelling deep, awaiting birth
they will tell you many things
they will bring you many dreams.

Mythical Creatures

I watched from my hiding place
On the ground
Behind small trees and hedges
Careful not to make a sound
And disturb an ethereal breakfast
Oatcakes and clovers
Honey and mead
No concern
For crumbs in soft manes

Fragrant flowers circled throats
I waited ensorcelled
While sunlight filtered down
Their gallop and prance
A beautiful earthquake
I felt the vibrations
Muscled flanks rippled
Hooves stomped

They paused their play
Sniffed at the air
One pushed a thick braid
Over his shoulder
Scanned the horizon, then turned
I held my hope and breath
His eyes caught mine
Head slightly cocked, then smiled

Are there rules
I asked - I needed to know
Run, play
Bathe in the sun
Stretch your limbs

Laugh and snort and dance and cry
There are no rules

I worried
I could not keep up.
But he held out a hand
Lifted me aloft
And I moved in space
While on his back
A wonderful, frightening feeling
You could never
Possibly imagine

Presently we stopped
I climbed down
We gathered in a circle
The females surrounded me
Petting me
And wove flowers
Through my hair

A flask of the sweetest mead
Was produced
Followed by
The dearest song
We drank and sang for hours
Until darkness

I never wanted the revelry to end
But I awoke alone in the moonlight
With only the empty bottle as proof
Of a day spent with centaurs.

Poetic Faith

There are conversations
In my head
I revisit
When I'm not strong
I use them
To support my theory
That I'm never quite enough

I'm being told
This has got to stop
I need to let it go
Those limitations
I impose upon myself

How is it
You see me
In ways
I never fully could
And how can I
Possibly translate
What you know

Into what I can become.

Leap of Faith

Quiver and tremble
down to the marrow
I'd always chosen safe
and secure until
one day I realized
I was done, and if I didn't
make changes fast
I would die having never lived
when I quit the corporate world
said goodbye to my security
they all shook their heads in disbelief
uttered gasps of incomprehension
you are no longer toeing the line
how will you? what will you?
I answered that I had no idea
as scary as that feels
every moment of every day
it is the most beautiful fear I have ever known.

All About Poems

Each time
I step to the edge of the cliff
and leap

Free-fall gracefully
or plummet like a stone
I never know which
until the flight is half over

So I repeat the process
foolishly and with delight

Again.

Beautiful Reminder

My willingness
Troublesome
This place
Filled with echoes
Full-voiced
Sounds of failure
Alone, my thoughts
Were too much
Drifting into desperation
Lacking safety and shelter
Prayer as years ebb
To a memory place
Not so painful

And then an angel
Masquerading
As a stranger
Gave me wisdom
I needed like sunshine

He told me so gently
One breath can just be

One single breath
My intention
It awakened
A joyous revolution
In my soul

Thank you
Beautiful reminder.

I wish

I wish
you peace

I wish
you didn't feel
so alone out there

I wish
things didn't feel
so impossible
so hurtful

I wish
there was some
word, promise, chant
that would bring you back
from the precipice you stand upon

I wish
I could tell you it would get better
and hold your hand,
and let you cry,
and be with you
and you'd wake tomorrow strong, refreshed, ready for all

I wish
I know feelings can be so
overwhelming, so cruel - I've felt them
I have stared down into that hole
I can only say that no matter what, I will love you
because you are of kind consequence, you are my sweet friend, and
you mean the world to me

I wish
I wish
I wish
Please, dear friend, please stay.

Fairy Tale

I was raised on
Fairy tales
A red book with
Delicate illustrations

If you told me
I could leap into those pages
I'd have jumped
Never looked back

Every night at Nana's
I could pick one
For her to read
Before prayers and sleep

She'd read my favorites
Again and again
Some that delighted
Others that frightened

Hundreds of pages
Delicious chapters
Smiling as she read to me
Her intent and attention mine

And those stories
What purpose did they serve
To dream, to wander into the fantasy
Confronting real-life fear and anxiety

Did it work - does it work
I try to understand where
Fairy tales and psychology converge

I only know they gave me

Rides on trusty steeds
Magical potions and mirrors
Uphill climbs to dragon's lair
Riddles to be solved

And once upon a time
I read them all on my own
And when I was a grown-up
I read them to my little girl

I didn't grow out of fairy tales
I'll never give them up
They still exist on the edge
Of my dreaming time.

My Body as a Fortress

I was built
With hope
Of withstanding harm
Brick by brick
Secrets contained
Inside my truth
In time - erosion
Leveled by grief
Walls crumbled
Battlements shifted
Cracks in a once
Impenetrable stonework chipped
Late at night, the manse
Settles with unease
Down steep staircases
Through dark hallways
Dreams echo
Keening baby, howling girl
Weeping woman, wailing crone
Gilded mirrors
Reflect remnants
What I am
Not always a shining victory
Nor grave disappointment.

Don't Let Them See

No matter what, I cannot
Let anything stop me
I desperately need
Whatever grace I can muster

I can't always prove my strength
Sure as hell not the best
Even in the best light

Today I am vulnerability
I peek out from
Eyes covered with splayed fingers
Don't let them see fears

I don't have to be the answer
Or fix a broken heart
But what if that heart is mine

I pound head and hands
Against walls
Utterly exhausted
And questioning worthiness

I long to be held safe in arms
Stronger than mine
And let love transcend pain.

New Beginning

The idea of a new beginning hurts
Because I am broken and not enough
I try and fail, try and fail
And the pattern continues
Until I'm left alone on the ground

The idea of a new beginning inspires
Because I am a soul who creates
I see everything, EVERYTHING
And I will keep searching
Until the universe says I am done

I exist as two beings
Inhabiting the same limited space.

Pretty Girls

The women on my mother's side
Were blessed with looks
Grace and lithesome ways
Modulated tones, and feminine features
Made for kisses by firelight
For reading romantic stories to sweethearts
Writing love letters to soldiers overseas
Never loud, never strident
Never too much, always just right
Anyone would agree
Such pretty girls

I resemble my father's side
Sturdy, no-nonsense bodies
Made for early mornings breaking ice
Hauling hay and feeding chickens in the yard
Large, rawboned farm women
Packed into a 5 foot 1-inch frame
A voice for shouting greetings from afar
Arms to comfort a crying child
Hands made for scrubbing floors and pulling weeds
Anyone would agree
I have a great personality

Dirt, under fingernails, hands stained with ink
Cracks in the skin and heart
Well aware of how I moved through the world
How I was perceived
Shy and awkward and never learned my place
I tried to ignore their orders
You can't - you shouldn't, you won't
I knew my soul and what it was worth
But longed for the fairytale

Anyone would agree
I'm a kindhearted lass.

Task Completed

I set my task
Without a thought
Never imagined
Heartfelt and heartbreak
Would be mine
Upon completion
Dig deep into soul
They said
Really wrench at it
Until it aches
Examine
All the hidden corners
Dirty secrets
Loving memories
Bravest struggles
Fondest wishes
And how, dear reader,
Will I live tomorrow
Not having this labor of love
To return to
Already I am
Mourning the emptiness
Task completed.

Anyone's Goddess

I have seen and done things
That tried to break me
It is written
On my face and body
I will never be anyone's Goddess
But I wanted to be yours
And I guess I wasn't
I think I would do
Nearly anything
Under the sun
To be seen by you
My love.

Trust in Dreams

I've walked
Strange lanes
In unfamiliar villages
Down drafty hallways
That stretch impossibly
With its wood twisting
In groans and cries
And entered rooms
Where giants wait
Or fields of flowers
Moss-lined garden paths
I've walked through forests
Darkly
Hidden from shadows
Bigger than they were meant to be
With scary teeth and hungry eyes
Voices barking in the wind
And only a candle to keep me safe
Then a big, deep sigh
With pounding heart
When I return to my pillow
My bed, my window, my room
I stretch like a cat
So grateful I am
And contemplate how I'd rather
Dream of love
Than live in a world without.

The Woman in the Mirror

If you didn't bother
You might not ever know
The me that I am
The one who lives inside
The one in my mind
My heart and my soul
External stuff might be jaded
Used and falling apart
Perhaps lacking
Relevance and grace
But that is not who I am
I am a traveler of galaxies and dreams
Of land masses unknown
And familiar neighborhoods
I am joy and light
I am pain and regret
I am thought and deed
My imaginings
Are multitude and dwell
Up with the stars
In the depths of dark oceans
Words are
Shallow, light, tender, forceful, and angry
They try to absolve
For the sins of my past and my future
For the wrongs I commit in this moment
I am happenstance and mercy
A jagged edge that cuts
Or a safe place for first aid
You can search my cellular destruction and scars
Or feel my empathy and willingness
To love all things in my universe
Do not discount me

Or ask me to hide in the shadows
Do not mistake me for invisible or weak
Or do
It is your choice
As this is mine.

Where the Creativity Flows

I know what's coming
There is silence
It is not peaceful, tentative, or light
What am I waiting for
And how long must I wait
A terrifying glorious revving of engines
Swirling and lifting and dispersing
Ears pop
Equilibrium and focus shift
I am sucked into the eye of the storm
I AM the storm

I know what's coming
I can't settle
On one thought
Or one plan
Everything in my world
Happens at once
Synchronous
Chaos and calamity
Ferocious whirlwinds
I am contradiction and outrage
Spiral and spin
Run hell-bent
Back to the beginning

I know what's coming
When the ancestors speak
Whispering secrets
For me to give to you
From me and you to us and them
They tumble out
Too quick to fathom

And one thought leads to another
Leads to an end
Or an answer
Leads to a solution
Leads to a problem

I know what's coming
Again, again
Go again
And keep going
Don't stop
My notions are the key
To every lock
I've tried to pick
Accelerated breaths
Excitement, creation, cool breeze
Ungainly
Lacking form and substance
Not just whole body and soul
But blood and bone
And seed and magic
And flame and desire

I know what's coming
Incantations created
Spells cast
Intentions set.

Dreams

It was recurring
I woke alone and afraid
Sweating and nauseous
I walked a wooded path
Held a lit candle, it was white

And protected me
From things
That caused me to scream
At the end of the path
Was a little old house
Upon further examination
It was revealed to me that this was the very
House of Hansel and Gretel's witch
I had unwittingly stumbled upon
But instead of a witch, the horror was
Someone who'd terrorized me
While I was awake
So wrong that he be allowed
In my dreaming life

I walked a wooded path
Held a lit candle, it was white.

I Walked a Wooded Path

I walked a wooded path
Held a lit candle, it was white.

I was a child
In a billowing nightgown
With feet bare
And wide, watching eyes
I crept along the forest trail
Long braids drifted down my back
Cool air whispered over my skin
I kept to the path
Protected by the light.

I was safe.

Magical
The one I needed most
Guided by my inner child.

See Me

See me.
Have I relevance.

Fading into the pale
Invisibility
How can
Something so transparent
Grow to be so massive
So all-encompassing
Obscurity in an obelisk
Or an oubliette
Claustrophobic
But also having
Breadth, depth, height, and width
And they would crow in delight to see me
Shrunk into their little box

No.
I have relevance
See Me.

International Women's Day

Witch,
Maiden, Mother,
Girl, Trollop, Bimbo,
Priestess, Miss, Crone, Whore,
Spinster, Wife, Harpy, Shrew, Daughter,
Sister, Wise-woman

Oh, you thought those names would hurt me
I wear them as a badge of honor.

Many have tried
To vanquish our fire.

We shall not be stopped.

All intentions focused on a future of true equality.
A safe haven for thought, body, and spirit.

Now we rise though the journey is rife with danger.

Come along or get out of the way.

We are bringers of life.

Sprout

The seed
a thought
that germinates
my mistakes
memories
escapades
the bits
and pieces
on the edges
of my brain
meld into a plan
I'm never quite sure of
that funny little process when
I lay in bed
on sunny and rainy
and windy mornings
and drift
beyond the notions
I plot and plan and devise
how I will do things
and make things
the part that is
the miracle
is when a feeling of rightness
settles over me
and I know
those disparate parts
will sprout
if lovingly tended
the idea is fully formed
awaiting execution.

Author's Note

If you've gotten this far in the book, you're very kind, brave, or perhaps it's a slow day. Whatever the reason, I thank you for reading my poems, buying my book, and taking a chance on me.

I never imagined I'd write anything, much less poems. It's all been a beautiful surprise. One I'll be grateful to for the rest of my life.

William Shakespeare, Robert Lewis Stevenson, Edgar Allan Poe, and Henry Wadsworth Longfellow were part of my very early childhood education. My mother memorized poems as a child and she taught me to love the sound of the words, rhyme, and cadence. Poetry was essential to her, and she passed that down to me.

This collection of poems are parts of me and things I've observed in my life, but also not of me. I feel inclined to describe what it all means, but I can't really. You may interpret as you will, and you should, with your own perspective guiding you. Yes, you will find darkness; with me, there always is a bit of sad, a bit of bleak. But you'll also find absurdity, joy, love, repentance, care, and thought. I am fascinated by the human condition, and if you're reading poetry, I think you are, too.

Lest you think I am some fragile flower, I am not. I am persistent with a twisted sort of sense of humor. You might have noticed little "Easter Eggs" in some of the poems. I put these in purely for my own amusement, never imagining that anyone would be as odd as I am.

From my heart –

AmyLee

Acknowledgements

I want to acknowledge the following people who have been so diligent and kind in helping me put this book together. Their love, support, and encouragement made all the difference; a more beautiful group of humans cannot be found.

Ticia Isom, Richard Holeman, Kerry Grant, James Mullen, Joshua Aitchison, Heather Wickers, Dannah A., Hank Dolworth, Shelly Bee, Pixie, and R.A. Steele.

Kat, of Katherine Magpie Design – cover design sorcery.

John de Vere – editor, friend, poet-wrangler.

About the Author

Whether it's raw verses filled with the grit of life and love, laments about lost family, or sacred offerings about the natural world, AmyLee writes with her whole heart. She has worked in the book and publishing world for decades and now spends her days learning the craft of writing and supporting independent authors as they refine their work.

AmyLee lives in the Foothills of California with her husband and cranky Chihuahua. She's a long-time member of the Sonora Writers' Group and has belonged to multiple book clubs over the years. She Co-Hosts a poetry show with Your Master's Voice on Twitter Spaces *The Poetry Show with AmyLee* and *Poetry is Sexy in Your Master's Voice*. You can find some of AmyLee's poetry and short fiction pieces at https://medium.com/@amylee_53969

www.ingramcontent.com/pod-product-compliance
Lightning Source LLC
LaVergne TN
LVHW041937070526
838199LV00051BA/2824